KW-054-547

Let's Make Music:
GCSE MUSIC PROJECTS

5 LET'S COMPOSE

Trevor Webb

Novello
London and Sevenoaks

Cat. No. 11 0213

Trevor Webb acknowledges the assistance and encouragement afforded him by the Kent County Council (Education Committee) in the preparation of this book.

LIVERPOOL HOPE
UNIVERSITY COLLEGE

Order No./Invoice No. £39 88
L6694 / 5315

Accession No.
268139

Class No.
372.78 T WEB   LCT

Control No.   ISBN

Total.
12/7/96

Let's Make Music: GCSE MUSIC PROJECTS

1: Let's Begin
   Cat. No. 11 0209   ISBN 0 85360 129 1
2: Let's Go On
   Cat. No. 11 0210   ISBN 0 85360 130 5
3: Let's Listen
   Cat. No. 11 0211   ISBN 0 85360 131 3
4: Let's Listen Again
   Cat. No. 11 0212   ISBN 0 85360 132 1
5: Let's Compose
   Cat. No. 11 0213   ISBN 0 85360 133 X

Teacher's Pack to include:
Books 1 – 5, Answer Book and Cassette
   Cat. No. 11 0214   ISBN 0 85360 134 8

Illustrations: PTA Creative Design, London.

THIS TEXT IS FULLY COPYRIGHT AND IS SPECIFICALLY EXCLUDED
FROM ANY BLANKET PHOTOCOPYING ARRANGEMENTS

© Copyright 1987 Novello & Company Limited
All Rights Reserved   Printed in Great Britain

No part of this publication may be copied or reproduced in any form or
by any means without the prior permission of Novello & Company Limited

Head office: 3 Primrose Mews, 1A Sharpleshall St.,
London NW1 8YL   Tel 071 483 2161   Fax 071 586 6841

Sales: 7 Vestry Road, Sevenoaks, Kent, TN14 5EL
Tel 0732 464999   Fax 0732 459779

Contents

TREVOR WEBB is Director of Music at Maidstone Grammar School, where he has been particularly concerned with the problems of encouraging teenagers to participate fully in class music. These books have been written as a result of the work done in classes for general music in the 13 – 15 years age-groups, with a firm emphasis on music making. The projects have been shaped towards the demands of the new examinations.

Before going to Maidstone he taught in schools of various kinds, and was for five years Lecturer in Music at Sittingbourne College of Education.

LIVERPOOL HOPE UNIVERSITY CC

To the teacher

LET'S COMPOSE provides opportunities for listening and composition on related themes. Each chapter presents the story of a descriptive piece and gives suggestions for compositions based on it. The widest possible range of techniques should be encouraged, using all available resources and going beyond the limitations of music alone to include dance, drama, and mime.

The work should end with the class hearing the composition which has provided the theme for the work.

To the student

Using music to tell a story or to describe something is nothing new. As far back as the sixteenth century William Byrd wrote a keyboard piece which he called *Mr Byrd's Battle*, and in this century Arthur Honegger composed an orchestral piece describing a steam locomotive, *Pacific 231. The Sorcerer's Apprentice*, by Paul Dukas, tells a story. These are only three examples from many.

On the following pages are outlines of stories to set to music.

1 Tam O'Shanter

A true story told in a poem by Robert Burns and in music by Malcolm Arnold.

'Against his wife's advice Tam, a wild Scotsman, has as usual spent market day drinking new ale with his friends. It is now night. Outside a tremendous storm rages. Tam sets off home, very drunk, on his horse keeping a lookout for the ghosts which haunt the nearby Alloway church, a place notorious for fatal accidents to travellers, for murders, and for suicides.

As he draws near he sees lights and hears the sounds of a noisy gathering. The drink has made him brave so he decides to investigate. He has stumbled upon a Witches' Sabbath. The witches are dancing to the sound of bagpipes, played by the Devil disguised as a big, black, shaggy mongrel. The coffins are open and the bodies are sitting up holding lighted candles.

On the altar are murderers' bones, the body of a hanged thief, five blood-covered axes, and five scimitars. The dancers are all grisly old men and women, save for one pretty girl dressed in her best petticoat, a 'cutty sark'. Tam is so excited by the dancing that he calls out 'Weel done, Cutty-sark!' Immediately all the candles go out. In terror he leaps on his horse and flees for his life, pursued by the witches who are led by the girl. He races for the bridge, because witches must not cross running water. As he and the horse jump to safety the witch seizes the horse by its tail, which comes off in her hand. So Tam escapes and gallops home to his scolding wife.'

Composing the music:

The wind blew as 'twad blawn its last;
The rattling show'rs rose on the blast;
The speedy gleams the darkness swallow'd
Loud, deep, and lang, the thunder bellow'd:
That night, a child might understand
The De'il had business on his hand.

ROBERT BURNS

Section 1: Tam riding off into the storm
    a) A 'tipsy' tune, sliding up and down. Tam keeping up his spirits and warding off the ghosts.
    b) Rhythmic sounds for the horse.
    c) Storm effects: white noise on a synthesizer; maracas, brushed cymbals etc.
Give the section a shape: A − B − C − A.

Section 2: The Witches' Sabbath
Hornpipes, jigs, strathspeys, and reels,
Put life and mettle in their heels.

a) A dance tune. Bagpipes: use *C* and *G* together to make a drone bass. Use *C D E G A* as the notes from which to make the melody. Choose an appropriate instrumental sound.

b) Creaking coffins and bones, blood-curdling shrieks, the Devil. Create sound effects with microphones, synthesizer.

c) Bring back Tam's tune to show his interruption, and end the section violently.

Section 3: The chase and Tam's escape
Tam roars out 'Weel done, Cutty-sark!'
And in an instant all was dark!
And scarcely had he Maggie rallied,
When out the hellish legion sallied.

a) Fast-moving patterns, perhaps several short ones repeated many times separately and together, with the horse rhythm from Section 1.

b) The witches: part of the dance tune, with added effects for the horses and the storm.

c) The jump: a short leaping passage; synthesizer or other sounds to describe the frightened horse.

Round off the whole piece with a **coda** (= a tail!) using grand victory music; big chords and a triumphant version of Tam's tune.

There are many ways of working out your composition. It can be a group effort; it could be done by one or two people using synthesizers and/or a computer. The piece can be made more dramatic by miming the story with it, in dance or drama. Can you turn it into a photographic slide presentation? Could you add a commentary – perhaps reading Burns' poem aloud?

You will have to decide how to preserve your work. A tape recording is easiest, but you may want to write parts down on paper. There is no need to use ordinary notation all the time; mix in your own symbols as well for things that cannot be expressed in a conventional way.

This story is well worth reading in Burns' setting. The English composer, Malcolm Arnold (b. 1921) has written a Concert Overture called *Tam O'Shanter*, with the different ideas represented by different themes. Listen to it, and compare it with your treatment.

- How has Malcolm Arnold evoked a Scottish atmosphere from the ouset?
- How does he show the storm?
- What instruments does he use to represent the drunken Tam and the horse, and how do they play?
- What does he do for the Witches' Sabbath?
- How is Tam's interruption illustrated?
- How do we know the horse has lost its tail?
- How do the witches vanish?
- Are conventional instruments used throughout?
- What advantages would electronic instruments give?
- Does the piece succeed in decribing the story?

2 The Pit and the Pendulum

This is the outline of a terrifying story by the strange American writer, Edgar Allan Poe. many of his stories have been made into films (for example, *The Fall of the House of Usher*), and there is a splendid musical interpretation of *The Pit and the Pendulum* in the *Turangalîla* Symphony (seventh movement) by Olivier Messiaen.

You awake in a dark prison cell, having been thrown there by the Spanish Inquisition. Trying to discover its size you slip and, when you regain consciousness, discover you are laying at the brink of a pit. By dislodging stones at its edge, you find it is immensely deep. A dim light shows the walls to be covered in frightening paintings of fiends and skeletons.

After eating what proves to be drugged food you sleep; when you wake up you find you are tied to a stretcher with only one hand free. Above you is a large, slow moving pendulum. It is gradually descending, and its bottom edge is of razor-sharp steel. As it swings it hisses through the air. Around you, lured by the smell of highly-spiced food, scurry rats.

Just as the blade is about to strike you break the ropes by means of smearing them with the food and luring the rats into gnawing through the bonds. The pendulum is suddenly drawn up into the ceiling and the rats hurry away.

The colours of the paintings begin to glow and you realise that the walls are being heated. As the heat increases so the walls slowly close in on you, forcing you to the edge of the pit and the waiting rats and water . . .

Composing the music:

Section 1: The march to the cell
> Solemn chord progressions (keyboards, brass, drums). Cymbal crash represents locking the door.

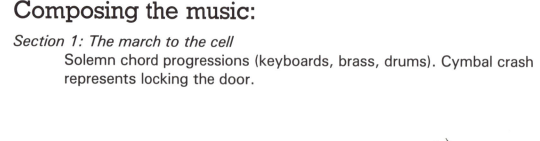

Section 2: Waking in the cell
  a) Wood blocks for pacing out the size of the cell.
  b) The pit: watery sounds, falling stones. There is a good sound available on one of the computers for this, but you should try to devise your own. Use high-pitched instruments, with short improvisations based on small groups of notes.
  c) The paintings: a xylophone for the skeletons? Short dance-like tunes over a simple chord pattern (perhaps a wholetone scale).

Section 3: The Pendulum
  a) Sleep music. Sliding cellos for snoring. (Listen to Britten's introduction to his opera *A Midsummer Night's Dream* for ideas.)
  b) Hissing sounds for the pendulum, getting louder as the pendulum descends. Use voices, bowed cymbals, white noise.
  c) Rats: scratching sounds, high pitched scurrying sounds (but be careful not to make this too much like the watery music in 2b).
  d) breaking free: triumphant chords, the rats and pendulum fading away.

Section 4: The walls
  a) Harsh chords for the return of terror, increasing in speed to represent the closing-in of the walls, and merging to form one sound.
  b) The end. Does escape come? Decide on what you want; it could be the fall into the pit, or it could be the sound of an avenging army.

Set about your composition in the same way as *Tam O'Shanter.* Remember that design matters. What you do must be clear to your listeners. Don't ramble!

Try a less formal piece as well, using sounds and tone colours to create an impression of the story. For suggestions on how to do this look at *The Flying Dutchman*.

LIVERPOOL HOPE UNIVERSITY COLLEGE

3 The Flying Dutchman

In this old legend a Dutch sea-captain, returning from the Indies with a rich cargo, tries unsuccessfully to round the Cape of Good Hope. After many failures he swears he will do it even if it takes him for ever. The Devil, hearing the oath, binds him to it, and condemns him to sail the sea for evermore, never finding a port.

The German composer Richard Wagner (1813 – 83), used this story as the basis for an opera plot. He made several changes, the most important being that once every seven years the Dutchman could land to try to find a woman to marry him. In doing this she would sacrifice herself, and death would set them free.

The Overture to the opera (*The Flying Dutchman*) has several very important themes; amongst them the Dutchman's theme, one for the heroine, one for the Devil's curse, and of course the storms at sea.

Composing the music:

Try two ways: a formallly designed piece, with clear themes; and a more atmospheric piece using small groups of sounds and notes to suggest the ideas. This piece could make use of improvisation and electronic sound effects.

1 A piece in rondo form.

Section 1: Introduction: a stormy sea (about 30 seconds long)
Rushing scales high and low, dramatic crescendi and diminuendi, brief snatches of a hornpipe tune getting submerged by the rest.

Section 2: The Dutchman (about 45 seconds long)
A big, sonorous and sweeping tune played on bold instruments. Simple harmonies, carefully planned phrases, and a singable tune.

Section 3: The Devil's curse (about 45 seconds long)
A short dramatic interruption, very loud and discordant. Use brass instruments if possible, together with thunder and lightning from the percussion instruments. Let it break into section 2 just before the Dutchman's theme ends.

Reproduced by permission of The British Library

Section 4: The Dutchman's theme returns
Section 5: The heroine (about 45 seconds long)

A contrasting melody, quiet and flowing, using more gentle instruments. Try to make it combinable with the Dutchman's theme, either whole or in part.

2 A sound picture.

Your aim is to use sounds and tone colours to create an impression of the story, rather than using tunes to identify the characters and events. Organisation is just as important as before!

a) Choose a conductor.

b) Divide the orchestra into groups, one for each idea to be represented. Groups here could be:

sea; ship; Dutchman; Devil's curse; heroine.

c) Decide on the instruments to be used in each. It is simpler to keep to one instrument per player.

d) Agree on symbols for the sounds to be made. For example:

Leave sounding until the sound dies away.

Cut off after x seconds.

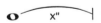 Repeat the note or sound as fast as possible.

 Improvise using these notes only.

Slide as the arrow shows (Name starting and ending notes if you wish.)

Single notes, spaced roughly as shown in the bar.

e) Prepare a blank score as shown here:

Duration in seconds	5	5	10	10	
Group 1 'SEA' Cymbal					Go on for as long as necessary
Bass Drum					
Group 2 etc.					

f) Decide by discussion who is going to play and where. Avoid having all groups playing at the same time except for very special effects or at the climax. Mark the places for starting and stopping on the score. Try to achieve a pattern:

Seconds	5	5	8	8	5	5
Group 1			←—————→			
Group 2	←————————→				←————→	
Group 3	←————→					←————→

and so on, with as many groups as you wish.

g) Each group will rehearse on its own, choose a leader to co-ordinate this.

h) The conductor will check each group and then combine them.

i) Record the finished piece and then discuss it:
  • How far does it achieve your aims?
  • Are the various groups keeping accurate time and entering and stopping in the right places?
  • Is there enough variety in tone colours and dynamics?
  • Is the design clear to the ear as well as the eye?
  • Does it make sense or does it ramble?
  • Could you understand what the conductor was telling you?

4 Count Egmont

Although these events took place more than four hundred years ago they are still relevant today.

Count Egmont, the Governor of Flanders, led the people of the Netherlands in a revolt against the tyranny of their Spanish rulers. The King of Spain, Philip II, sent the Duke of Alva to crush the revolt in 1567.

Alva tricked Egmont into a meeting, wherupon Egmont was taken prisoner, being executed in the main square in Brussels in 1568. Eventually however the Dutch succeeded in overthrowing the hated Spanish rule.

The story was made into a play by the German writer Goethe. Between 1809 and 1810 Beethoven composed incidental music for this play, and the Overture is an important piece in today's orchestral concert programmes.

Beethoven   Goethe

Composing the music:

1   A piece using conventional melodies and chords.

Section 1: Introduction: the oppressed people of the Netherlands
Solemn and dramtic chords, timpani rolls.

Section 2: The Hero
A tune to represent Egmont.

Section 3: Arrival of Alva and the Spanish army
Military music.

Section 4: Egmont's capture and execution
Set up a conflict of sections 1 and 2, leading to a march to the scaffold: solemn funeral melody and rhythms with slow muffled drum rolls.

Section 5: The Dutch victory
Change the key; use Egmont's theme in a more joyful style.

2   Using the same scheme compose a sound picture using the techniques described in *The Flying Dutchman*.

3　Below are the main themes used by Beethoven in the overture. Expand them, alter them to suit your ideas, and work them up into your version of the story.

Introduction:

Egmonts theme:

Music to suggest Spain:

(This is a dance rhythm from Spain, and Beethoven's listeners would have been familiar with it.)

Victory music:

4   Write a short piece for singers, actors, and band.
    Main characters: Count Egmont (the hero); Duke of Alva (the villain); Captain of the Guard; Executioner; Spanish Army; Dutch citizens.
    A possible plan:
    a) Short instrumental introduction to set the scene.
    b) Curtain up on a Dutch market place. Spanish soldiers are bullying the people. Egmont enters and sings a song calling the people to revolution.
    c) The Spanish army arrives to suitable military music. Alva leads them, singing a boastful song about how he will take and kill the rebel leader.
    d) Egmont is captured and led away; music to reflect the Spanish jubilation and the Dutch sorrow.
    e) Execution scene: a mime to funeral music.
    f) Dutch attack on the Spaniards, who are driven away: music and mime. A final song of victory.

Beethoven's Overture

The second part of the eighteenth century had seen the rise of a new musical design, now called 'Sonata form'. The basic idea was to present several different themes contrasted in style and key. One or more were worked out musically as fully as possible. The opening ideas were than played again either fully or in part. A concluding passage (a coda) usually rounded off the music. One of the important features about this plan was the way in which the music travelled from its home key to a number of different keys and then back to the home key. The plan proved so adaptable and so useful for dramatic compositions that it has remained one of the most important musical designs ever since.

Some of Beethoven's themes have been quoted already. Listen to the whole overture, following a score if possible. When you are quite familiar with it answer these questions:

* Does the plan help to make the ideas of the story easier to follow or not?
* Do you need to know anything of the story to enjoy the music?
* What differences are there between the various themes?
* Can you understand the music better because you know the plan used?
* Do you enjoy the music more because you know the plan used?

5 Petrushka

Petrushka is the hero of a ballet by Diaghilev, who was the director of the Russian Ballet, with music by Igor Stravinsky. It was composed in 1911.

The story is the classic one of two men in love with one woman, but in this case all three are puppets. It begins at the Shrove-tide Fair in Admiralty Square, St Petersburg (now Leningrad) in the year 1830. Amongst the roundabouts, organ grinders, dancers and the crowd of sightseers, is a little theatre.

The showman appears, and with a tune on his flute and a drum roll the puppet show begins. The three puppets are Petrushka, the Moor, and the Ballerina, and they are brought to life by the Showman and then perform a vigorous Russian dance.

In the second scene we are inside Petrushka's room. He has been thrown in after the show, and is intensely unhappy because his love for the Ballerina is not returned as she finds him so grotesque. As he dances sadly the Ballerina passes through on her way to visit the Moor.

Scene 3 takes place in the Moor's room. He is a splendid figure, elaborately dressed and very conceited. As he dances he tries without success to cut a coconut in two with his sword. When the Ballerina arrives he attempts equally unsuccessfully to join her elegant dance. Petrushka comes in, full of jealousy, and is forced out by the Moor.

When the curtain rises on scene 4 we are back at the fair. A noisy crowd is joined by a man with a dancing bear. Suddenly there is a violent commotion from the puppet theatre as Petrushka rushes out, chased by the Moor who kills Petrushka with his sword. The Showman calms the crowd by explaining they are only puppets, but as the people disperse, leaving the Showman alone, Petrushka's ghost appears, and the frightened Showman runs for his life.

Composing the music:

Choose one of the following sections and compose a sound picture, first by improvising and then by preparing a graphic score. (The way to do this is explained in 'The Flying Dutchman'.)

Section 1: The fairground
- a) Roundabouts
- b) Dancers
- c) Popular songs
- d) Organ grinders
- e) Crowd noises
- f) Street sellers

A player will be needed for each item. Allow each to come into prominence before all combine for a loud finale which is interrupted by the Showman.
Use some popular tunes.

Section 2: Petrushka's room

A slow, sad dance tune. Try improvising over this ostinato bass played on a bass xylophone, metallophone or pizzicato cello:

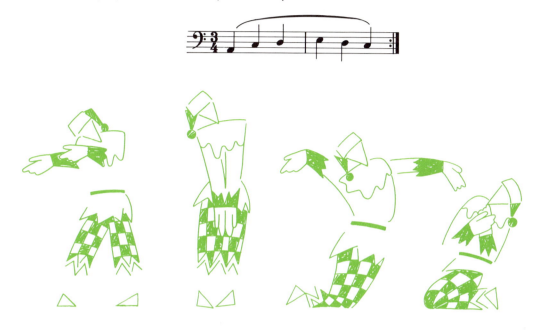

Add a recorder or other wind instrument, developing this as the dance tune:

The Ballerina enters, and the dance becomes faster:

Combine the two tunes, and break off as the Ballerina vanishes into the Moor's room.

LIVERPOOL HOPE UNIVERSITY COLLEGE

Section 3: The Moor's room

Improvise a dance over this rhythm:

Make the tune sound dignified, but with a hint of things going wrong.

Section 4: The murder

Use the melodies of Petrushka and the Ballerina, and the Moor's rhythm, working out a chase. Add electronic effects if you can. End with the Showman's flute and drum, and a ghostly appearance of Petrushka's theme (put through an echo chamber?).

Stravinsky's music

The ballet music is enjoyable on its own, though made much more exciting by the dancing and staging. Stravinsky divided the story into scenes as above. In the Fairground scene he uses traditional Russian tunes as well as a popular song from a musical of the time, about a lady with a wooden leg. Listen to the music scene by scene, and consider the following questions:

- What means does Stravinsky use to convey the atmosphere? (For example, the excitement and bustle of the Fair, the elegance of the Ballerina, the clumsiness of the Moor, the pathos of Petrushka?)
- How important is the orchestration to the success of the music? Would it be as effective played on a keyboard alone? How would it respond to being treated in a pop style?
- Does the music need the dancing and staging to reach its full effect?

6 Romeo and Juliet

Shakespeare's plays have been the inspiration for many pieces of music. Mendelssohn wrote music for *A Midsummer Night's Dream* in 1826, and in 1959-60 Benjamin Britten wrote his opera based on the same play. Verdi wrote his opera *Macbeth* in 1847, following this with *Othello* in 1887 and *Falstaff* in 1893. *Romeo and Juliet* has inspired a Concert Overture by Tchaikovsky (1870), a ballet by Prokofiev (1935), and a musical by Leonard Bernstein, *West Side Story* (1958), as well as many other pieces.

In sixteenth-century Verona there lived two noble families, the Capulets and the Montagues. For generations there had been a bitter feud between them, with bloody street battles a regular occurence.

One evening the Capulets held a masked ball, to which the guests would come disguised. Romeo, Montague's son, and two friends, decided to go, uninvited of course. There Romeo met and fell in love with Capulet's daughter, Juliet. Knowing their love to be hopeless they marry in secret. Juliet returns to her home. After the wedding Romeo meets his friends, only to find them engaged in a street fight with Capulet supporters. One of them, Tybalt, kills Romeo's close friend Mercutio, and he in turn is killed by Romeo.

As a result, Romeo is banished from Verona. Juliet meanwhile has been told she is to marry a young nobleman, Paris. In despair she returns to the Friar who married her and Romeo, and he gives her a sleeping draught which will make her appear to be dead. She drinks it on her wedding day, and is taken away to be buried.

The Friar sends a message to Romeo telling him to come and rescue her, but unfortunately the news reaches him earlier by another friend. Romeo, believing Juliet to be dead, hurries to her tomb in Verona. Finding Paris watching her 'body' he kills him and then commits suicide.

As he lies dead, Juliet wakes up and sees the two corpses. The two families arrive, summoned by the town police, but Juliet has already killed herself with Romeo's dagger. In remorse for all that has happened the families heal the rift between them.

Composing the music:

Choose one of the following sections and make a sound picture. You might like to do as Bernstein did and bring the whole story into the present day or you could use an old style. Decide beforehand which you intend to use. Work by improvising short sections and then prepare a graphic score.

Section 1: The masked ball and the meeting of Romeo and Juliet

    Work out a short dance theme; if you are using a present-day setting try a disco-style theme and rhythm. If you use an old style experiment with modal tunes (i.e. keep to the white notes only of the piano keyboard). Compose themes for Romeo and Juliet, making them contrast so that they are easily recognisable, but also make them capable of being played together.

Section 2: The secret wedding

    Use a hymn-like tune (or borrow a genuine one), and make up a wedding march. You could use fragments of the one by Mendelssohn, which begins thus:

    Link the two themes of Romeo and Juliet to represent the marriage.

Section 3: The street fight

    Use percussion instruments only together with voices. Lots of noise and confusion. Incorporate electronic sounds, especially distortion, if you can.

Section 4: The tomb scene

    Use the themes of Romeo and Juliet, but changed to make them as tragic as possible, perhaps by playing them more slowly, changing the octave in which they are played, and changing the instrumants used. Bring in muffled drums and again use voices singing solemn chants.

Add a mime to each scene or read/act the appropriate scene from the play as you perform the music:

    Section 1: Act 1 scene 5.
    Section 2: Act 2 scene 6.
    Section 3: Act 3 scene 1.
    Section 4: Act 5 scene 2 (this will need shortening).

Time the music so that it and the action relate properly to each other. On your graphic score show exactly where specific actions take place. (For example, Romeo's and Juliet's first meeting, Mercutio's death, and so on.) It will be very important to give exact timing for the events.

Your composition can be extended by taking other scenes from the play and illustrating them in the same way.

Tchaikovsky's Overture

This is a Concert Overture; in other words, it does not come before an opera or play (like Beethoven's *Egmont* Overture or Wagner's Overture to *The Flying Dutchman*). It is like *Tam O'Shanter* in that it depicts some of the main events of the story and is a piece of music which stands on its own. Tchaikovsky takes some of the most important happenings, and uses either definite themes (as for the fight, the love scene, and the Friar who marries the lovers), or music which sets a mood, such as the slow beginning to the Overture and the dramatic and solemn end. As you listen to the Overture ask yourself these questions:

• What orchestral effects does Tchaikovsky use to convey the various ideas?
• Can you think of a better way?
• Is there a clear musical design?
• Do you need to know the design, the story, to enjoy the music?

    Now go on to hear (and see, if you can) Leonard Bernstein's version. Think critically about the two and form your own opinions as to their relative merits.

Published by Novello & Company Limited
Printed in Great Britain by Superprint Ltd., Lewisham, London

268139

This book is to be returned on or before
the last date stamped below.

MARKLAND LIBRARY
Tel. 737 3528

BECK LIBRARY
Tel. 737 3601

Telephone Renewals can only
be accepted after 4.30 p.m.

LIBREX

WEBB.T.

268139

LIVERPOOL HOPE
THE MARKLAND LIBRARY
HOPE PARK, LIVERPOOL, L16 9JD